Vincenzo Sguera / Michele Moricci

Natural Pop
GRAPHICS
vol 1

Creative Research
for Graphic Designers, Artists and Stylists
205 Designs ready to use freely

Published by
ARKIVIA BOOKS srl

Via Provinciale, 68
24022 Alzano Lombardo
Bergamo (Italy)
Phone and Fax:
(0039) 035515851
web:
www.vincenzosguera.com
www.arkiviabooks.com
e-mail:
info@vincenzosguera.com

The DVD included is free,
it is an integral part of this
publication and cannot be
sold separately.

Copyright © 2009 Vincenzo Sguera

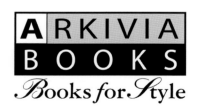

Copyright terms

The use of graphics included
in this book and in the DVD is free.
The copyright of graphics belongs
to the owner, who does not transfer
an exclusive use.
Include a line, indicating the copyright
credit, everywhere possible.
The republication of this book in part
or in whole and with any kind of
medium (paper, CD, DVD, Internet etc.)
is forbidden except by a reviewer who
may quote brief passages in a review.

The creation of graphics is
a continuously evolving activity.
Any resemblance between the designs
in NATURAL POP GRAPHICS VOL.1
and other designs subject
to intellectual-property copyright
results from ignorance
of the existence of said copyright
or is purely coincidental.

If, unknown to the authors and/or
publisher, any design contained in
this book is already registered,
they do not authorize the use
of such design by book buyers.
They decline all responsability since
they cannot be aware of all the designs
registered or used previous to this
publication in all countries.

SOME EXPLANATIONS on COPYRIGHT

All the designs in this book are ready
for production and the use is free.
This is really important:
Those who buy this book can use freely
the designs inside with only 3 reserves:

1 - they may not use the designs to produce
    a book with the same purpose and may
    not sell the designs in internet website.

note: they may sell their products derived
from these designs but not the designs
themselves

2 - they must respect the destination of
    the designs.
    So if a design is a texture, a different use
    is not authorized, such as a trademark;
    the same is valid for characters or graphics
    suitable for printing on T-shirts
    These designs are merely ornamental designs.

3 - Mention the copyright © *Vincenzo Sguera*
    where possible.

Copyright belongs to Vincenzo Sguera
who in this case cedes the use,
apart from the reserves mentioned.

Thus, these designs are
not "copyright free" but "use free".

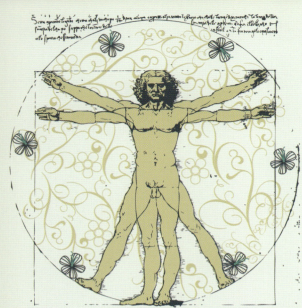

DVD *info*
technical details

The Book contains 1 FREE DVD with 5 FOLDERS, suitable for WINDOWS® and MACINTOSH®

TYPE OF FILES
The Files contained in the FOLDERS AI/EPS are all VECTOR :
this means in the first place that they can be opened by all softwares that use VECTOR Design.
It is made up of exact lines that delimit areas where the color is uniform.
This enables the design to be brought to any size while retaining the maximum quality required.
The Files contained in the FOLDER PDF and the FOLDER JPG are all BITMAP .

SOFTWARE
The main VECTOR softwares are :
ILLUSTRATOR (the first came out in1988), CORELDRAW and FREEHAND.
The BITMAP files (FOLDERS 4-5) can be opened in software such as PHOTOSHOP, CORELPAINT, PAINTSHOP, COREL PAINTER etc..

SIZES
The files are all real size 100%.

COLORS
In VECTOR files the single colors are flat, without transparencies or shading off.
By changing the Four Color percentages they can be modified within the software.
Each single color can be saved to prepare films, calenders, looms.
The colors used are at the most 8.
The background color, even if white, has been counted and also any color which is repeated in the design.
In BITMAP PDF files the colors are in "Four Color Process Printing", that is CMYK. meanwhile the JPG files are in RGB.

There are 5 FOLDERS and each one has a different format and contains the same 205 graphics
but with different characteristics.
In total there are 1025 Files

FOLDER AI v.10
These Files are in AI Format saved for Illustrator 10.

FOLDER AI v.5
There are all the designs with the same characteristics as FOLDER AI v.10 but saved for ILLUSTRATOR 5.

FOLDER EPS v.5
These Files are in EPS Format saved for ILLUSTRATOR 5.
Being a old format, it is useful for people that have old versions of ILLUSTRATOR or FREEHAND or CORELDRAW.

FOLDER PDF 600dpi
For those who want to have BITMAP Files
in PDF PHOTOSHOP Format,
600 dpi and CMYK, they are in this FOLDER.

FOLDER JPG 150dpi
Here you can find Low Resolution BITMAP Files
in JPG format (150 DPI in color scale RGB),
that can be used to develop projects with lighter Files
to speed up work and are for quick vision.

All files can be opened by:
· ILLUSTRATOR 5 and following
· CORELDRAW 8 and following
· FREEHAND 8 and following
· PHOTOSHOP in any version.

Warning:
to avoid possible production problems with the vector files, I suggest you deactivate the overprint option, because the colors are flat and are not overprinted.

The copyright of WINDOWS, MACINTOSH, ILLUSTRATOR, CORELDRAW, FREEHAND, PHOTOSHOP, CORELPAINT, PAINTSHOP, COREL PAINTER belongs to the owners.

NPG0001

NPG0002

NPG0008

NPG0009

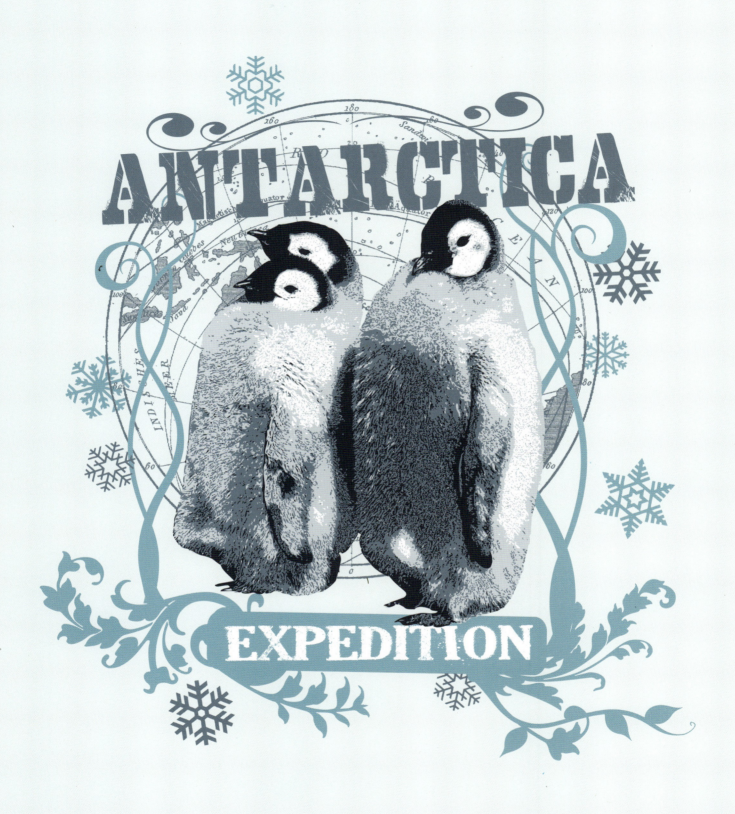

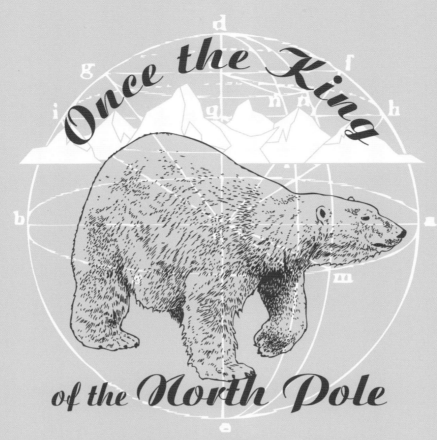

NPG0011

NPG0012

NPG0013 ○ ● ● ●

a country of the Kingdom of Denmark
located between the Arctic and Atlantic Oceans,
east of the Canadian Arctic Archipelago

NPG0014 ○ ● ●

Area: 317 km2. Highest elevation: 1230 m
(State President Swart Peak, Marion Island)
One small ice-cap (1% glacierized)

NPG0015

NPG0016

NPG0020

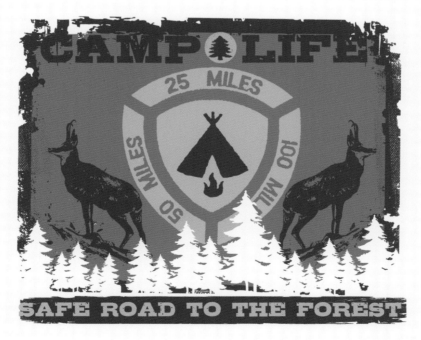

NPG0021

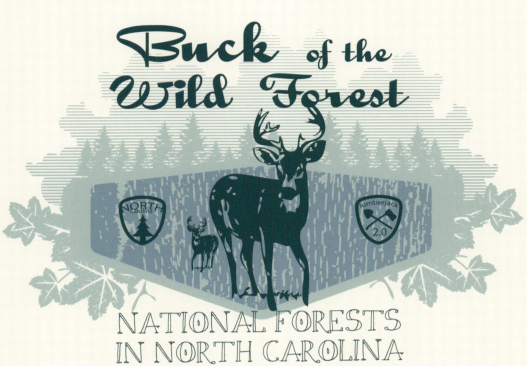

NPG0022

NPG0023

NPG0026

NPG0027

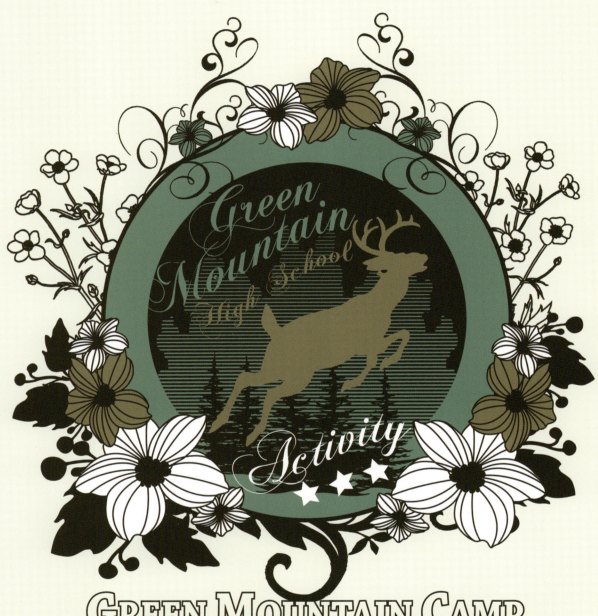

NPG0030

NPG0031

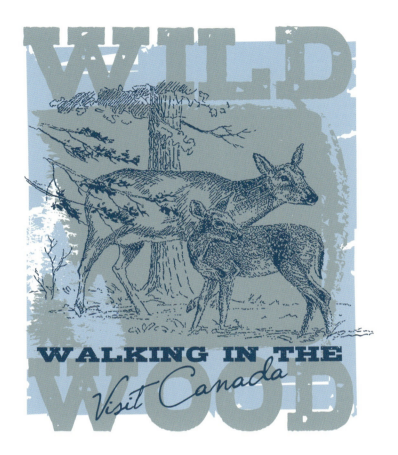

NPG0032

NPG0033

NPG0035

NPG0036

NPG0037

NPG0038

NPG0040

NPG0041

NPG0046

NPG0047

NPG0048

NPG0049

NPG0050 ○ ● ●

NPG0051 ● ● ● ○

NPG0052

land of the coupling game...

NPG0053

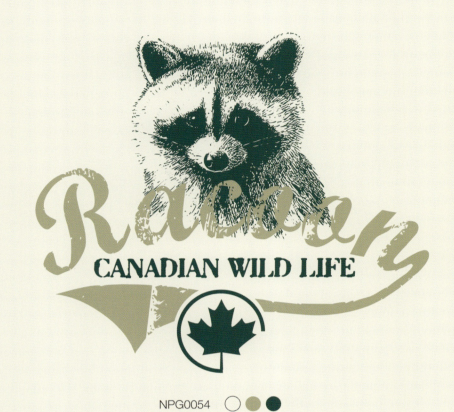

NPG0054

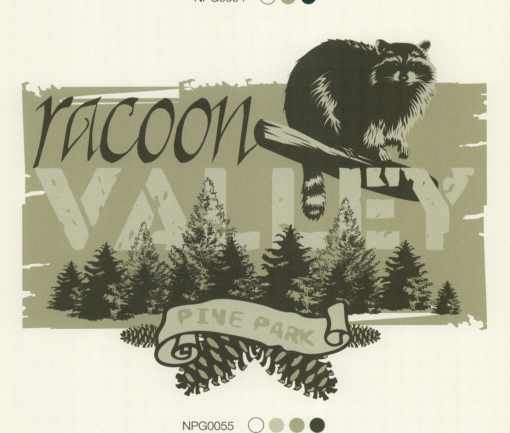

NPG0055

NPG0057

NPG0058

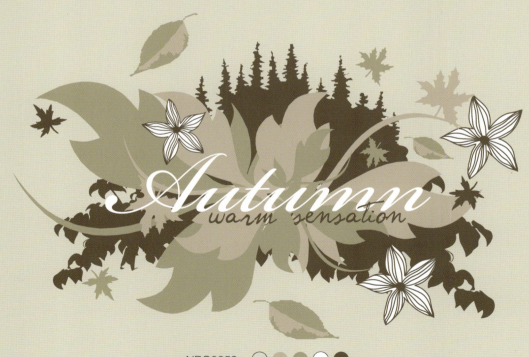

NPG0059

NPG0060

NPG0061

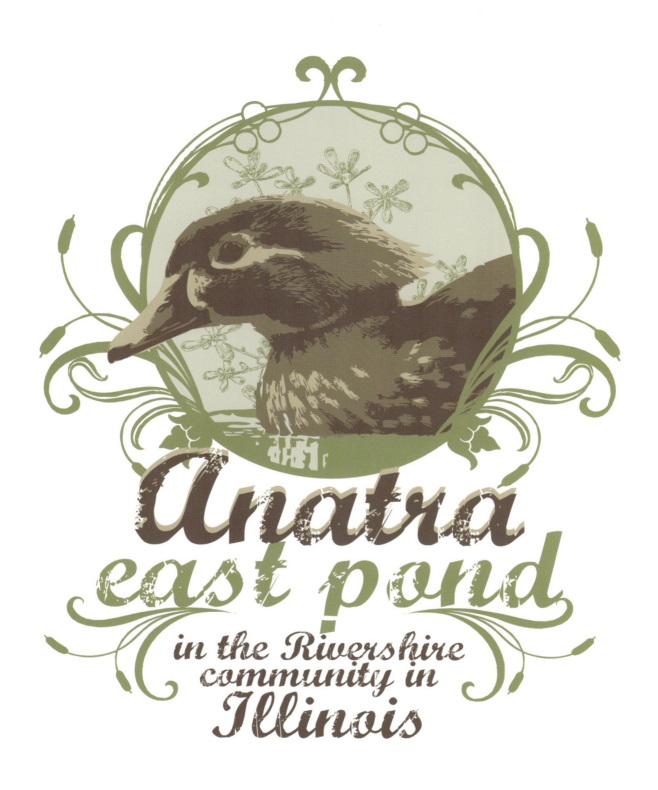

NPG0062

NPG0064

NPG0065

NPG0066

NPG0067

NPG0070

NPG0071

NPG0072

NPG0073

NPG0075

NPG0076

NPG0079

NPG0080

NPG0082

NPG0083

NPG0084

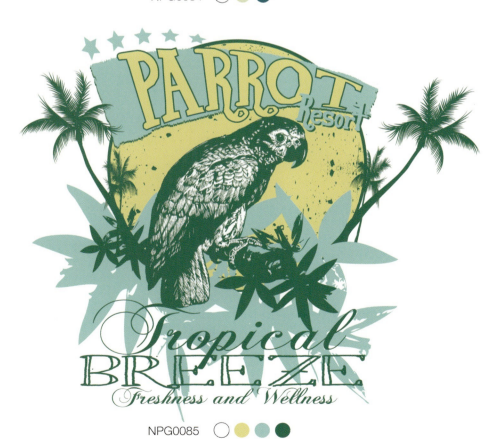

NPG0085

NPG0088

NPG0089

Page 059

NPG0090

NPG0091

NPG0092

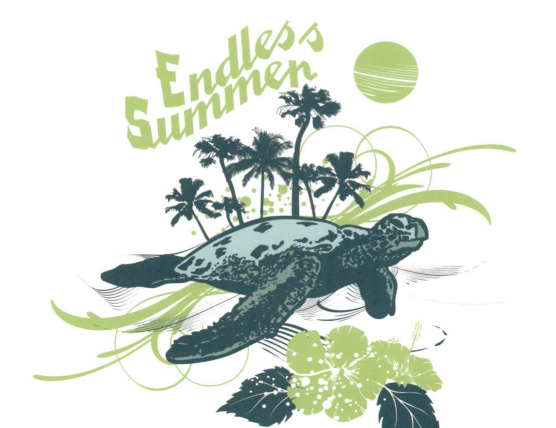

NPG0093

NPG0095

NPG0096

Page 063

NPG0097

NPG0098

NPG0101

NPG0102

Page 067

NPG0103

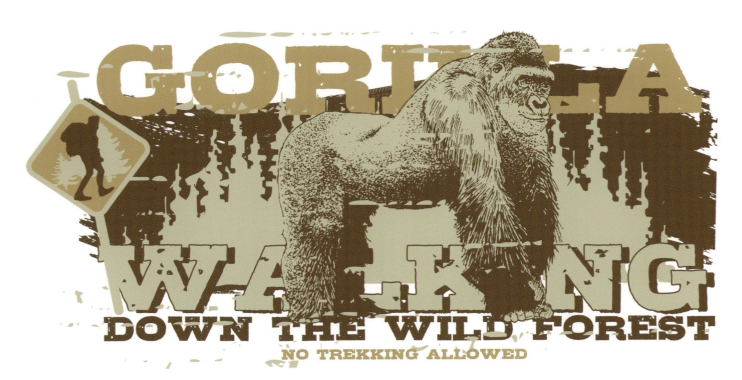

NPG0104

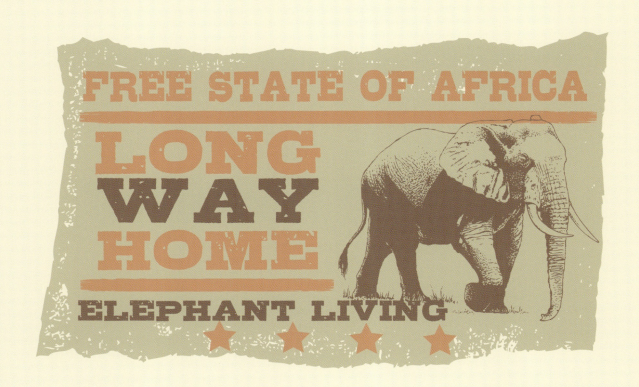

NPG0106

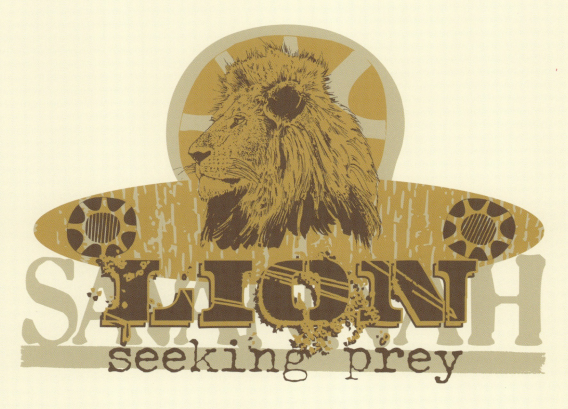

NPG0107

NPG0110

NPG0111

NPG0113

NPG0114

NPG0117

NPG0118

NPG0120

NPG0121

NPG0124

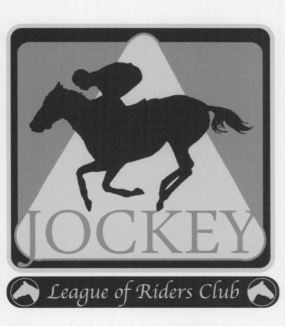

NPG0125

NPG0126

NPG0127

NPG0128

NPG0129

BOTANIC GARDENS
Royal Academy of Plants

A Farm Town where you can find honey, liquors, propolis, bach flowers, day and night creams and all cosmetic products with officinal plants.

NPG0130

NPG0131

207 Upper East Side - Manhattan - NYC

NPG0132

NPG0133

NPG0134

NPG0136

NPG0137

NPG0138

NPG0139

NPG0142

NPG0143

NPG0145

NPG0146

NPG0148

NPG0149

NPG0155

NPG0156

NPG0157

NPG0158

NPG0160

NPG0161

NPG0167

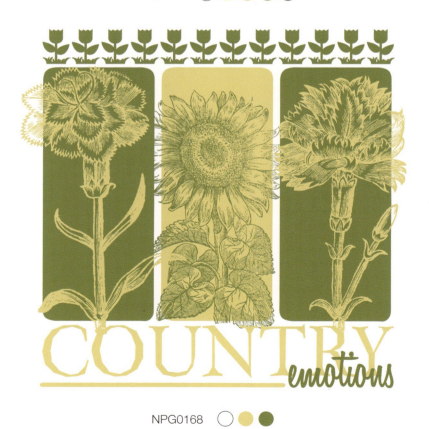

NPG0168

NPG0171

NPG0172

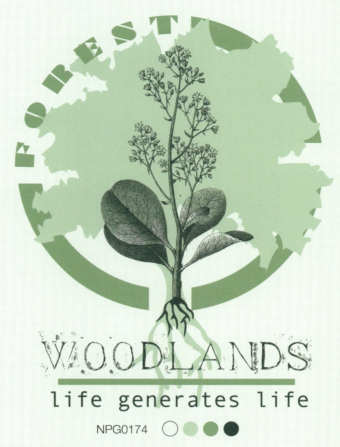

NPG0174

NPG0175

NPG0180

NPG0181

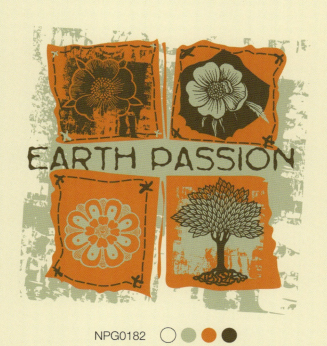

NPG0182

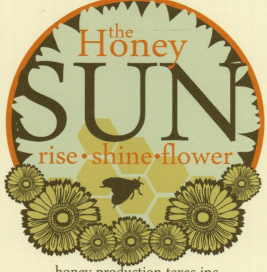

honey production texas inc.

NPG0183

NPG0184

NPG0185

NPG0186

NPG0187

NPG0190

NPG0191

NPG0192

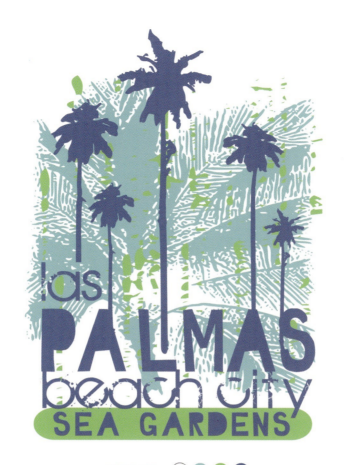

NPG0193

NPG0194

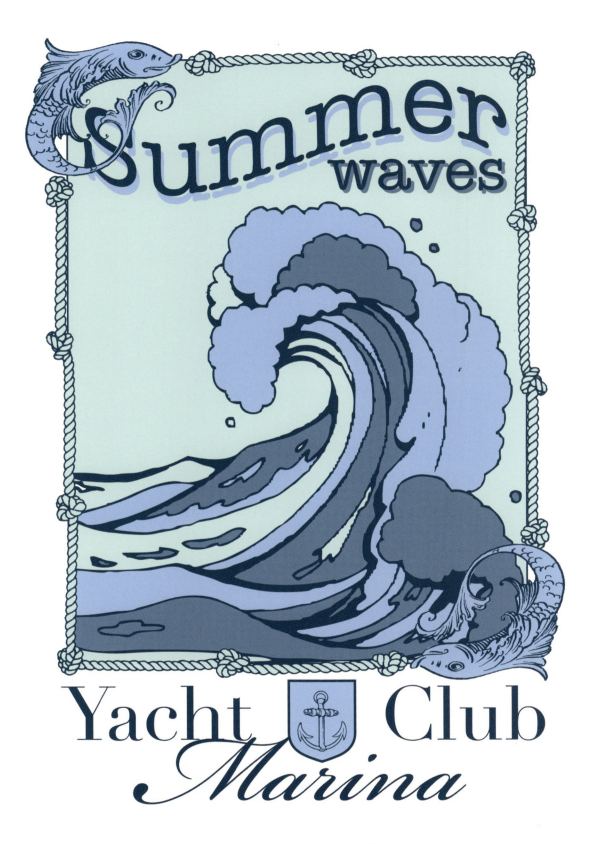

NPG0198

NPG0199

NPG0200

NPG0201

NPG0204

NPG0205

• a new series

Vincenzo Sguera
Character Styling vol ❶

• the Cat •

This BOOK, the first of a NEW SERIES has an ambitious objective:
TO DEVELOP NEW CHARACTERS, FREE TO BE USED.
AT THE SAME TIME IT CAN TEACH HOW TO CREATE THEM.

Each title will develop one theme at a time: cat, cow or penguin etc. but with different ways of characterizing them.
I will show how to construct the basic forms, the psychological and chromatic characteristics. Like any respectable Character, they will have a suitable **NAME** and **LOGO**.
I include a large series of **MODEL SHEETS** which show how to move and animate the Character in various positions and situations. I have also added **GRAPHICS**, **LOGOS** and **TEXTURES** with the characters developed.

• • ALREADY AVAILABLE

Characters — These are some examples of model sheets included in this book. At first the front and side positions and then many interesting developments.

candycat · choco · jazu · jobi · neo · pinxie

© 2008 Vincenzo Sguera

| ISBN 9788888766096 | HARDBACK • 72 pages size 24cm x 30.7cm | With the book a useful CD is included with all images ready for use and can be modified with most software. |

AVAILABLE IN JUNE 2009

Characters

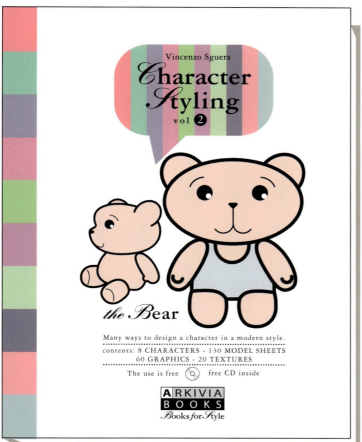

Vincenzo Sguera
Character Styling vol ❷

• *the Bear* •

This BOOK is the 2nd of a new series.
I have increased the numbers of Characters to 8.
The model sheets in this case are a bit fewer.
The GRAPHICS and TEXTURES linked to each
Character remain unaltered in number.

I wanted to develop more Character ideas to offer
a wider choice of use and stylization.
For each one I will show how to construct
the basic forms, the psychological and chromatic
characteristics.
Also these Characters will have a suitable NAME
and LOGO.

I include MODEL SHEETS, GRAPHICS, LOGOS
and TEXTURES with the Characters developed.

ISBN
9788888766133

HARDBACK • 72 pages
size 24cm x 30.7cm

With the book a useful CD is included with all images
ready for use and can be modified with most software.

Smiling Faces part 1 — Character n.12

012MOD08
012MOD03
012MOD01
012MOD06

Bunnie's Holiday

Character n.01

001MOD16

001MOD10

001MOD11

001MOD13

001MOD14

STYLING BOOK vol 1
FARM and WOOD CHARACTERS

ISBN 9788888766034
HARDBACK • 144 pages
size 24cm x 30.7cm
Already Available

Contents:
16 Families of Characters
with 229 Developments
in 16 Model Sheets,
plus Modular Patterns,
Logos and Accessory Lines.
A Free DVD is included.
All are Free for Use
and Ready for Production.

The 16 families of characters have been developed all in a fresh and modern style. Real model sheets can be used for graphic needs.
You can move parts of them to create other positions since they are created in Adobe Illustrator with separable parts (body, arms, head, eyes etc).

The logos, the scenes and the textures developed are in flat colors, but can be changed into CMYK.

Vector files are suitable for WINDOWS®-MACINTOSH®

005MOD12

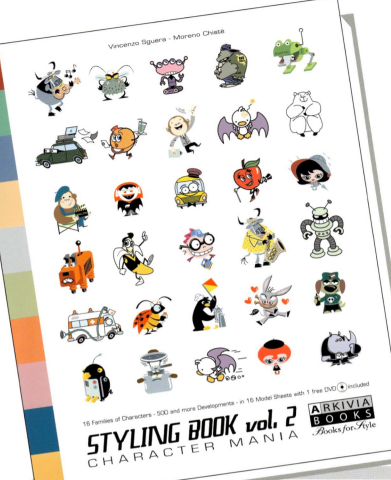

STYLING BOOK vol 2
CHARACTER MANIA

ISBN 9788888766058
HARDBACK • 144 pages
size 24cm x 30.7cm
Already Available

Contents:
16 Families of Characters
with 500 and more Developments
in 16 Model Sheets.

A Free DVD is included.
All are Free for Use
and Ready for Production.

The 16 families of characters have been developed all in a fresh and modern style. Real model sheets can be used for graphic needs.
You can move parts of them to create other positions since they are created in Adobe Illustrator with separable parts (body, arms, head, eyes etc).

The model sheets developed are in flat colors, but can be changed into CMYK.

Vector files are suitable for WINDOWS®-MACINTOSH®

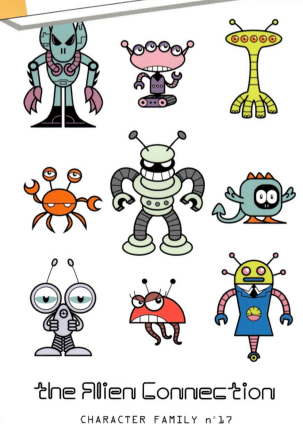

the Alien Connection

CHARACTER FAMILY n°17

Town & Country Cars

CHARACTER FAMILY n°29

© 2008 Vincenzo Sguera

Black and White Matrix 2

ISBN 9788888766164
HARDBACK • 144 pages
size 24cm x 30.7cm
Publication Date: Autumn 2009

275 TEXTURES saved in 5 ways
1375 files in all
1 Free DVD included
for WINDOWS and MAC
Vector and Bitmap Files
Ready for Production
The use is Free

This time, the colours of black are tinged with things, objects, people, animals, all scattered and overlapping to generate a modern style of textures. A brushstroke of freshness, no half-tones or hesitation.
Lines, silhouettes or synthetic images develop single themes, entering by right into the world of decoration.

They can be used with many graphic softwares, such as ILLUSTRATOR or PHOTOSHOP.

Available in Autumn 2009

Matrix Graphix 1

ISBN 9788888766157
HARDBACK • 144 pages
size 24cm x 30.7cm
Publication Date: Autumn 2009

250 GRAPHICS saved in 5 ways
1250 files in all
1 Free DVD included
for WINDOWS and MAC
Vector and Bitmap Files
Ready for Production
The use is Free

250 graphics in black and white, charged with style.
A bit 80's Pop, with a dark and punk atmosphere.
This sort of culture seems to live again today contaminated by gothic fluorescences.
As in the textures, in these graphics too the colours that black possesses can be seen in all the nuances of soul. They can be used with many graphic softwares, such as ILLUSTRATOR or PHOTOSHOP.

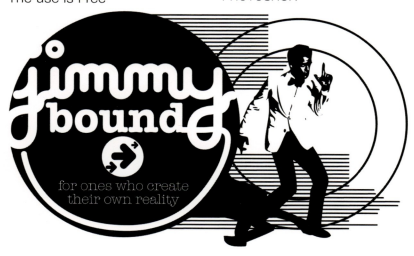

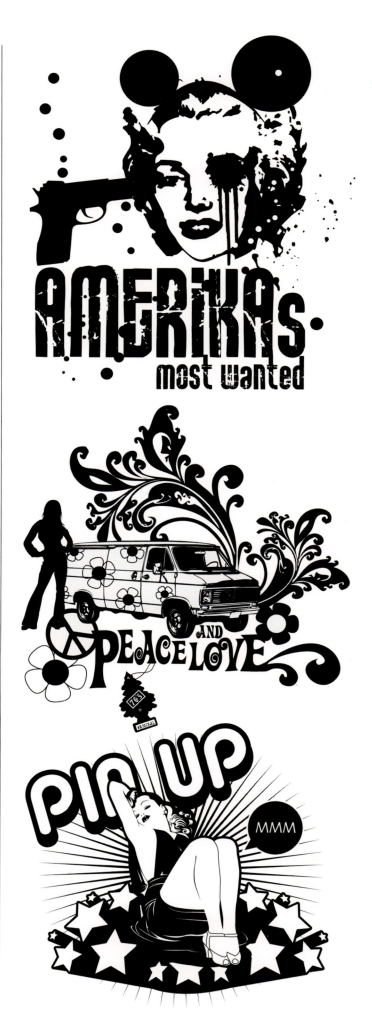

Already Available

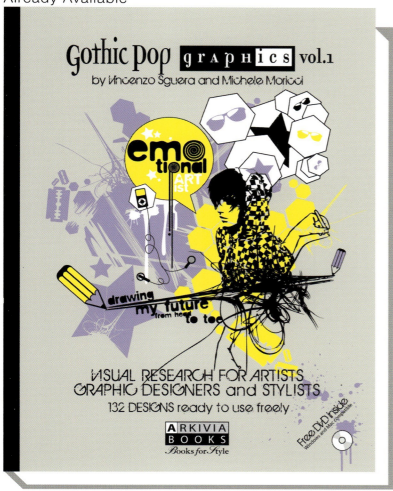

gothic pop graphics vol. I

132 Designs in 3 color variations saved in 5 ways
1980 files in all ready to use freely.

Prints and Logos for all sorts of use, in the style that characterizes the "ten years style" of this century.
A flow of creativity in counterpoint to the past from which it freely culls elements in a fluid and artistic way.

ISBN 9788888766102 HARDBACK • 144 pages size 24cm x 30.7cm	1 Free DVD included for WINDOWS and MAC Vector and Bitmap Files

ISBN 9788888766089 • ALREADY AVAILABLE • HARDBACK • 144 pages • size 24cm x 30.7cm • 1 free DVD included

Vincenzo Sguera
JUNIOR POP
T E X T U R E S
vol ❶
Visual Research for Artists
....
Graphic Designers and Stylists

200 Modular Patterns
with **1** free CD 🅞 included
for WINDOWS and MAC
Vector files
Ready for Production

ISBN 9788888766041 • ALREADY AVAILABLE • HARDBACK • 144 pages • size 24cm x 30.7cm